MEDIA MAGIC

ANNE ROONEY

Belitha Press

First published in the UK in 2002 by
Belitha Press Limited
A member of Chrysalis Books plc
64 Brewery Road, London N7 9NT

Text by Anne Rooney
Editor: Susie Brooks
Designer: Peter Clayman
Illustrator: Woody
Consultant: Lisa Murphy, Fawcett School
and Homerton College, Cambridge

ISBN 1 84138 439 9

British Library Cataloguing in Publication Data for this
book is available from the British Library.

Printed by Eurolitho S.p.A, Milan (Italy)

Some of the less familiar words used in this book
are explained in the glossary on pages 46 and 47.

CONTENTS

Dear Reader

What's your room like? Stuff all over the place – on the floor, under the bed, stuffed in drawers? (Mine too!) Bet you're always being told to tidy it up 'so you can find things when you want them', aren't you? Well, whether or not you think that's a good idea for your room, putting your writing or computer project in order will make it much whizzier and more impressive.

No one thinks in order – but if you put everything down just as you first thought of it, your work would be hard for anyone else to follow. In fact, it would probably be hard for even you to follow a day or two later!

That's what this book will help you with – sorting out the jumble of brilliant ideas you've got and getting the most from the info that's at your fingertips. If you want to make a poster to get people to come to your play, wow your class with your super presentation or build a website for your club, read on to find the best ways of getting people to take notice.

INTRODUCTION

Have you ever thought about how a conductor in an orchestra must feel? To make beautiful music instead of a dreadful racket, he or she has to get all the musicians working at the same time, playing the right notes in the right order.

That's a bit like what you have to do when you write a project or work on facts and figures. There's all this mess – words, numbers, pictures, ideas – and you somehow have to tell them what to do and put them in their places. Sometimes you have to make all this out of – nothing! You're not given a pile of words to sort out, are you? You have to go away and think of them, and then put them in the right order.

IT'S A FACT
Do you have trouble keeping things in order? Perhaps you've got a problem with entropy! That's the name for the habit things have of getting more and more disorganized, or chaotic.

words

numbers

Things aren't very good at getting into order themselves. So, master of the universe – time to take control!

SORT YOUR THOUGHTS!

Have you ever tried brainstorming? No, it's not having a tantrum – it's putting down everything you can think of about something to get you started on a project. You can brainstorm on your own or with other people. It's a great way to start work, especially if you're stuck for inspiration.

Brainstorming is easy. You just write down all your thoughts – however silly – on a piece of paper or a whiteboard. You'll end up with a right jumble of good bits and bad bits – some truly brilliant ideas and some that are so silly they make you laugh. You can brainstorm ideas about how to present your work as well as what you're putting into it.

> I said brainstorm, not rain storm!

Don't panic if your ideas look a real mess at first – your thinking is supposed to be messy! You can sort it all out afterwards.

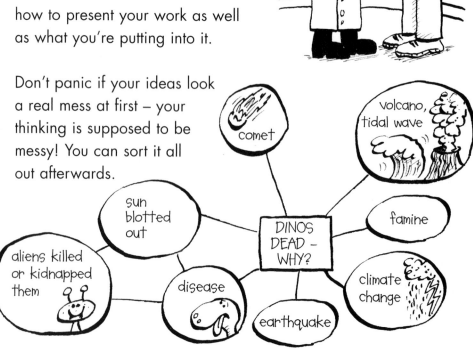

comet

volcano, tidal wave

sun blotted out

famine

DINOS DEAD – WHY?

aliens killed or kidnapped them

disease

climate change

earthquake

ORDER, ORDER...

The way you sort out your ideas will depend on what you're trying to do. Is it something that needs to go in a particular order? If you're trying to give instructions, they probably need to go in a sequence from the start to the end.

If it's a list, you might want the most important things at the start. Or maybe sequence isn't important but you need to bring out key points and make people notice them, or show the relationship between different bits of information.

First five only!

Please can I have:
felt tip pens
tangerine
batteries
for my CD
player
ruler
note pad
new
bike

BE A REPORTER

If you've got a school report or project to put together, you need to turn your brilliant jumble of a brainstorm into an ordered set of facts or a reasoned argument. You'll need to:

What happened to the dinosaurs?

— think of a title that tells people what your report's about.

Dinosaurs lived for 165 million years but then they all disappeared about 65 million years ago. What happened to them? There are several theories to think about.

— start with a short introduction that says what you're going to talk about.

Deadly meteorite?

Some people think the dinosaurs were wiped out when a meteorite struck the Earth. It would have caused earthquakes, tidal waves and volcanic eruptions. The climate would have changed and the sun might have been blocked out by dust in the air.

....
....
....
....

— work out what the main things you want to say are. Put these in order – maybe the most important first, or the most exciting, or the one that naturally comes first if it's a sequence. Write a section or a paragraph for each main idea.

My verdict

The sky did it! Most of the evidence I've looked at makes me think a meteorite probably wiped out the dinosaurs – but we may never be completely sure.

— end with a summary or conclusion that draws together your main ideas or your decision on what you're writing about.

So – start, middle and end – easy, isn't it?

PROCESS THOSE WORDS!

The brilliant thing about writing your work on the computer is that you can make it better and better without having to write it out all over again. You can put your thoughts down in a bit of a jumble and move them all around afterwards, check your facts (and your spelling!) and make it all OK before you hand it in.

Make sure you know how to do these things with your word processor:

★ cut and paste bits of text – that's moving parts of your work around, or even from one document or file to another.

★ check the spelling – get the spell checker to do it for you, but read it through, too – it's not as smart as you are and it won't spot correctly spelt words that are in the wrong place.

★ use Find and Replace to change a word – so if you wrote 'comet' when you meant 'meteor', you can change all comets to meteors in one go.

★ add page numbers – just in case you drop all the pages on the floor and jumble them up.

IT'S A FACT
The spell checker might say some things are mistakes when they aren't – it doesn't usually recognise names, foreign words and some abbreviations. So you need to check the spell checker's spelling, too!

Stop! No comets, sorry – meteors only!

JAZZ IT UP

If you've used a word processor or a desktop publishing program for your report, you can jazz it up by using different text styles, sizes and colours, arranging the text between the margins and adding pictures, lines, boxes and shading.

What happened to the dinosaurs?

Dinosaurs lived for 165 million years but then they all disappeared about 65 million years ago. What happened to them? There are several theories to think about.

Deadly meteorite?

Some people think the dinosaurs were wiped out when a meteorite struck the Earth. It would have caused earthquakes, tidal waves and volcanic eruptions. The climate would have changed and the sun might have been blocked out by dust in the air.

My verdict

The sky did it! Most of the evidence I've looked at makes me think a meteorite probably wiped out the dinosaurs – but we may never be completely sure.

Look at your toolbar menus and buttons to find ways to:
★ change the colour, size and font (lettering style) of your text.
★ move your words to the middle of the page, or to the right-hand side.
★ add lines, boxes and shading.
★ put in pictures.
★ make lists with numbers or bullets (shapes like blobs or stars) at the start of each line.

IT'S A FACT
You can make your own pictures using a computer painting program, scan in drawings, or use photos from a digital camera. If you don't have these, try clip art — ready-made pictures you can get on CD or from the web (see page 46).

EYE CATCHING

Spend some time thinking about how to grab people's attention. You need to use your imagination as well as your computer for this! Think about how you're going to make people take notice.

I've lost my dog. Have you seen her? Call 701351.

LOST DOG

Please help me find Sparky. She's a cute brown and white mongrel with a long, feathery tail. Last seen on 7 December (her birthday) chewing a bone outside the Post Office. Please contact Sadie on 701351.

HELP, I'M LOST!

I got lost outside the Post Office on 7 December. If you find me, please call Sadie on 701351 and say you've found Sparky. There will be a reward!

The first sign doesn't even give the vital info – no one's going to find this kid's dog. The second is fine – as long as you don't fall asleep reading it. But the third's got something extra to make people take notice – and maybe even look for the dog.

11

PICTURE PERFECT

It's always worth thinking whether you'd do better to put in a picture or add loads of words. You might be able to use a photo or a diagram instead of describing something – it makes your work look more interesting and it may give a better idea than what someone imagines from your writing. (But if you're writing a story, imagination may be better than a picture!)

IT'S A FACT
In a scary story, a description of a monster is often much more effective than a picture. That's because we all imagine the monster that's scariest for us. The monster the artist draws might not be at all frightening for some people.

If you want to describe a process or instructions, a diagram might be easier to follow and more interesting.

How babies work

Some diagrams you can do on your word processor. Others you might find easier in a computer drawing program. And some will just be easiest hand-drawn on a piece of paper – though you could scan them in and add them to your work, or print out smart labels to stick on them.

TIMES TABLE

In writing, you don't always need sentences and paragraphs. Think about how to make your information easiest to understand.

Sometimes, tables are the best way to show info. They help people to compare facts, and to take in lots of information at a glance. Use your word processor to add a table, setting the number of rows (lines across) and columns (lines down) that you want. Put titles for the rows and columns to show what's in them, if you need to. Don't forget you can use colours and cool borders and you can put pictures in your table, too.

Animal	Lives in	Eats	Size
	garden, hedgerows	slugs, worms, fruit	20 cm
	house	cat food, mice, birds	60 cm
	earth	decaying plant matter	10 cm

Numbers are usually much easier to deal with in rows and columns. Can you imagine your bus times being written out in a paragraph? Complicated! That's why they're printed as a table.

No 11 buses leave at 08:15, 08:45, 09:15 and every half hour until 23.00 (except on Sundays) from outside the Post Office; they go past the school 5 minutes later, then 11 minutes after that they get to the shops, then...

No 11

Post Office	School	Shops
08:15	08:20	08:31
08:45	08:50	09:01
09:15	09:20	09:31
09:45	09:50	10:01

13

FIGURE IT OUT

If your numbers show a pattern or need to be compared, you can do better than a table – you can draw a graph or a chart. There's no point in drawing a graph of bus times, but if you've measured the temperature in your room or weighed your tortoise on and off for a year, a graph will help you to see a pattern in the results. Your spreadsheet program can probably do this for you.

You'll need to:
★ put in all the numbers – the computer can't do that bit!
★ choose which numbers you want to put in your graph.
★ choose the type of graph you want.
★ pick labels and how you want the divisions on the axes.

Suppose you've weighed your tortoise, but haven't done it very regularly. A table like this won't tell you much:

Date	Weeks I've had Tor2	Weight (g)
13 May 01	0	80
03 Jun 01	3	90
24 Jun 01	6	105
22 Jul 01	10	125
19 Aug 01	14	145
11 Nov 01	26	155
20 Jan 02	36	195
17 Feb 02	40	220
14 Apr 02	48	300

But draw a graph (see next page) and it will show you exactly how your tortoise has grown.

BAR, LINE OR PIE?

You can make lots of different kinds of graph with your computer. You need to pick the right type for the info you're showing.

A bar chart or a line graph is good if you want to show a trend – for example, how fast your tortoise grew or how your heart rate changes as you exercise more and more.

Growth of Tor2 the tortoise

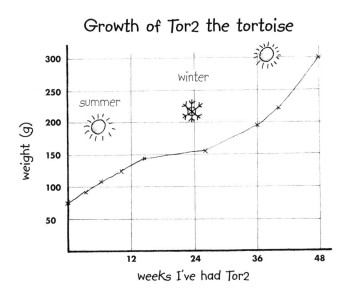

A pie chart is a good way to show percentages or proportions – you've probably done one to show the eye colours of kids in your class, for instance. Use a pie chart if you can split up your info into clear categories – such as blue, brown, green, or rainy, sunny, cloudy.

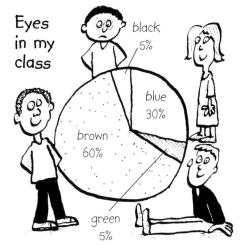

Eyes in my class

black 5%

blue 30%

brown 60%

green 5%

15

PILE 'EM HIGH

Pictograms are another fun way of charting information. You might be able to do them on your computer, too. Instead of a boring old column, you use pictures to show the proportions – much more fun to look at. A pictogram's better for showing trends in information than exact numbers as you have to stop and count how many pictures there are.

Pets owned by kids in my class

	cats	dogs	hamsters	mice	porpoises
7			🐹		
6			🐹		
5	🐱		🐹		
4	🐱		🐹		
3	🐱	🐶	🐹		
2	🐱	🐶	🐹	🐭	
1	🐱	🐶	🐹	🐭	🐬

IT'S A FACT
The info you get out of the computer is only as good as that you put in. Check you're putting in the right stuff. Maybe that porpoise should have been tortoise?

You might be able to use your own pictures or clip art for the columns – have a look in the options or Help for the program you use.

Number Crunching

Sometimes the info you've got is just the start of something bigger. You might have a lot of figures you've collected, maybe from a survey or from the Internet. How do you get something more interesting from them? You can use your brain and the computer to work on your raw data (that's facts and figures you haven't done anything with) and cook up some interesting info.

raw meat

raw data

IT'S A FACT
A bit of data is a fact or figure that you haven't done anything with yet. Information comes from processing — that's working with — data.

Data Dealing
The simplest way of using data is to compare facts. Here are two bits of data: Luki is 108 cm tall; she is six years old. If you looked at a growth chart and compared Luki's height to other children's, you'd find out the info that Luki is short for her age.

Luki

NEW FACTS FOR OLD

If you've got some bits of data, you can often make new info from them. Here are some facts from a book:

Only two people a year are killed by sharks.

About 30,000 people are killed by snakes each year.

There are about 5,000 million people in the world.

About two million people die of malaria, carried by mosquitoes, each year.

With a bit of calculation, you can find these new facts:

1 You're 15,000 times more likely to be killed by a snake than a shark.

2 One in every 2,500 people dies of malaria each year.

3 Your chances of being killed by a shark next year are one in 2,500 million.

4 Mosquitoes are more dangerous than sharks.

5 If you lived until you were killed by a snake, you might live 166,666 years and eight months!

Using a computer, you can work with figures quickly, finding totals, averages and percentages and carrying out all sorts of other sums. You can put lists into order, sort them into groups and draw graphs from them. If you have facts that aren't numbers, you can pick out trends and links between them.

Super Spreadsheets

A spreadsheet is the best way to work with numbers. It saves loads of time because once you've put all your numbers in and told it the sums you want to do, the computer just gets on with it. If you change any numbers it'll work out new answers – magic! Let's have a look at a spreadsheet for Tor2 the tortoise.

	A	B	C	
1	Date	Week	Weight (g)	
2	13-May-01	0	80	
3	03-Jun-01	3	90	
4	24-Jun-01	6	105	
5	22-Jul-01	10	125	
6	19-Aug-01	14	145	
7	11-Nov-01	26	155	
8	20-Jan-02	36	195	
9	17-Feb-02	40	220	
10	14-Apr-02	48	300	

Each cell – little box – holds a number, a text label or a formula (a formula is an instruction for working out a sum). So far, there are only numbers and words in the cells. But we could add a formula to work out how much Tor2 has grown. It would need to calculate: final weight – starting weight.

Tor2's final weight is in cell C10 and his starting weight is in C2. To make the spreadsheet work it out, we'd need to type the formula: =C10–C2 into a cell. The spreadsheet would do the rest, coming up with the answer: 220 (g).

In a spreadsheet, you can use
+ to add numbers   – to subtract
* to multiply   / to divide
Every formula must start with '='.

Fact Factory

What if you've got all kinds of bits of pieces of info – not just numbers? Don't worry, you'll still be able to get the computer to do some of the work for you. This time, you need a database. It lets you store, sort and mess around with text, numbers, dates and all kinds of other info.

A database is a bit like a box of cards with info on. Imagine you have a set of 'digi-pij' trading cards that you swap with your mates. Each one has a picture of a different diji-pij, its name, and bits of info about it, such as where it comes from and what it can turn into or do.

DIGI-PIJ (Digital Pigeons)

71

Name: Cryptobeak
Size: 90 cm
Flock: Secret
Attack: Cryptoclone – copies enemy's info bank and encrypts it so the enemy can't use it
Power rating: 6,000

This is just one card – there could be hundreds to collect and each would have info about a different digi-pij.

If you wanted to find all your digi-pij with a power rating of more than 400, or all those from the Secret flock, you'd need to look through all your cards and sort them out. You might decide to keep them in order in a box – but you could only put them in one order. So you might put them in order of name, A–Z. That would make it easy to find a particular name, but hard to find, say, card number 136.

Sometimes you need to be able to sort your info quickly.

SMART SORTING

A database is like a smart box for keeping your cards in. It can re-order the cards instantly, and look through them to find information. It can even count them and do calculations.

In a digi-pij database, there'd be a 'record' for each digi-pij, and each record would have a 'field' (a space to fill in) for each piece of information – so there'd be a field for the name, a field for the power rating, and so on.

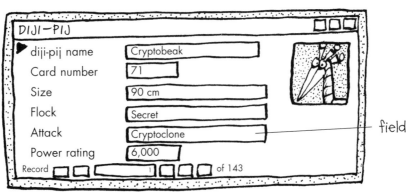

diji-pij name — Cryptobeak
Card number — 71
Size — 90 cm
Flock — Secret
Attack — Cryptoclone — field
Power rating — 6,000
Record — 1 — of 143

DIJI−PIJ

You could get the database to sort your digi-pij in order of name, card number, size – or by flock and then by name (eg A–Z of Secret Flock, A–Z of MegaPower Flock). You could ask it to find all the digi-pij taller than 60 cm, or with names that have an 'x' in. It could work out the average power rating of all your digi-pij, or find how many have the letter 'q' in their Attack field.

CHECK IT OUT

While it's a great idea to get the computer to do your work
so you can spend more time having fun, don't forget to check
it's done it properly! If you don't give quite the right instructions,
it can come up with a totally off-the-wall answer. Remember, the
computer's not smart – it's quick and it doesn't get bored, but
if you ask it to do slightly the wrong thing, it won't realise.

So take a quick look at the answers it comes up with, estimate
what you think the answers should be, and if there's a big
difference do a bit of detective work to find out who's got
it wrong. You need to check that you've put the right data
in and given the computer the right instructions.

IT'S A FACT

When companies blame
'computer error' for
things like sending you
a gas bill for a million
pounds even though you're
only nine, or getting
stroppy with dead people
because they didn't turn
up for school last year,
it's really because people
either put in the wrong
data or didn't tell the
computer what to do
with it properly.

22

SCREEN SCENE

You don't always need to present your work on paper – why not show it to people on screen? You could make a website, a slide show or a multimedia display. For any one of these, you can use all you've learned about styling text and using tables, charts, pictures and diagrams, but you can add even more, like sound and video and linked bits and pieces, too.

WICKED WEBSITES

There's lots of software you can get to help you build a website, and quite a bit of it is free. Whatever you use, you'll need to:

★ work out what you're putting on your website, and what's going on each page.
★ get together all the pictures and words you need.
★ choose the colours, text styles, buttons and backgrounds.
★ collect any sound and video you want to use.
★ draw up a plan showing how you're going to link from one page to another.
★ make up all the pages.
★ link the pages together.
★ check to make sure it works.

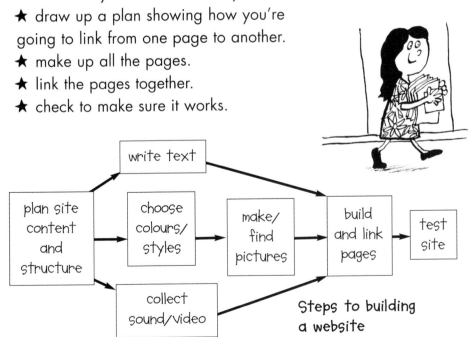

Steps to building a website

WEB WEAVERS' TIPS

Make sure your website works well
by following these simple rules:

★ keep all your pictures and
pages in a single folder so the
links are easy (unless your site
is really big).

★ give all your pages and pictures
short names with no spaces in – stick
to eight letters if you can.

★ use the same fonts on all the pages –
it looks neater and stops people getting distracted.

★ unless you use colour coding for different parts of your
website, use the same colours on all pages, too.

★ use the same buttons for the same purpose each time
so people don't get confused.

★ make it easy to find your way around so people don't get lost.

★ don't put the same information on more than one page – use
links instead – that way you only have to make a change once
if you need to alter it.

NOW PRESENTING

Making a presentation sounds pretty
scary, but it doesn't have to be.
Standing up and talking in front
of everyone in class isn't the
only way to do it – you could
do your presentation as a
slide show people can look
at on screen. You might still
need to present it – or they may
get to go through it on their own.

My scary
presentation –
Ghosts in our Town

24

SLIDE SHOW

If you make a slide presentation with a program like Microsoft PowerPoint, you can print it out to pin to the wall or use with an overhead projector – or you can show it on the computer. That way, you don't have to be around to present it – you can send it to someone else on a floppy disk or even put it on a website.

The cool thing about doing your presentation on screen is that it can include all kinds of whizzy things – sound effects, moving pictures, music, video, text that moves around – you can't do that with an overhead projector!

PRESENTATION TIPS 'N' TRICKS

If you're doing a presentation on the computer, here's how to make it really cool:

★ don't put too much text on each slide! The text should be quite big so it's easy to see and should cover your main points – if you need to say more on a particular topic, add another slide.

★ keep your slides lively, with pictures and diagrams, lines, arrows, boxes, sound and moving cartoons.

★ try some special effects, like slides fading into one another or appearing from the side of the screen. But don't use lots of different ones – you don't want to confuse people!

★ look out for menu options like 'transition' (that's how one slide changes to another), 'effects', and 'animation' (which makes your text or pictures appear on the slide one after another).

★ pick a colour scheme, buttons, text styles and slide designs and stick with them – your presentation will be easier to follow if all the slides have the same basic design.

Tooth trouble?

Right, let's take a break for a story. Maybe this will give you some ideas for your next school project!

Dear toothfairy

Can u spare a minute to anser sum queschins for me? I am doing a shcool progict on bisnisses and I want to rite about your bisniss moddle.

How much do u make each week?

Do you get the same munny for all teeth?

What happnes to u if not enuf teeth fall out?

What do u do with all the teeth u get?

Do u do anything els xsept collect teeth?

Can I have more for big teeth than littul wons?

Thanks.

Love Max

Dear Max

Thank you for your letter. Unfortunately the tooth fairy in your district can't read it (she comes from abroad and only understands correct English). Also, tooth fairies in this country are required by the Education Department to encourage you to learn to spell. Please write your letter again, using a word processor and checking the spelling.

Thank you

Area supervisor

Dear tooth fairy

Can you spare a minute to answer some questions for me, please? I am doing a school project on businesses and I want to write about your business model.

1. How much money do you make each week?
2. Do you give the same money for all teeth, or can I have more for big teeth than little ones?
3. What happens to you if not enough teeth fall out?
4. What do you do with all the teeth you get?
5. Do you do anything else except collect teeth?

The Area supervisor tells me you come from abroad. Do you speak any other languages? And are foreign tooth fairies allowed to get a job anywhere, or do you need a permit to work here? Why did you leave your own country? Weren't there enough teeth? (I'm not being rude – I like you being my tooth fairy – I just thought it would be useful to put it in my project.)

I look forward to hearing from you.

Love

Max

IT'S A FACT
You can make a numbered list with your word processor and the numbers will stay in the right order even if you move the things in the list around.

Dear Max

Thank you for your letter. I am happy to answer your questions – no one has ever written a project about me before! I hope you will let me see it when it's finished.

Here is the information you wanted:

1. I make about 30 euros a night.

2. We give the same money for all teeth unless someone asks for more. You might think this is cheating, but we like to encourage people to think for themselves, so there's a bonus for showing initiative. You can't get more than 3 euros for a tooth in this area. For that, it has to be a good quality molar – that's a back tooth – nice and clean with no fillings. Since you've asked, you can have more for big teeth than little teeth! The rate for you is now 1 euro for incisors (that's small teeth at the front), 2 euros for canines (those pointy ones that come next) and 2.5 to 3 euros for molars, depending on condition. (So don't eat too many sweets, clean your teeth at least twice a day and visit your dentist regularly.)

3. We try to save some money for a rainy day – that's a day when not so many teeth fall out. It is not true that we pull teeth out, or make them wobbly in the night – that's just a nasty rumour. After all, there's the same number of teeth in the end so it wouldn't do us any good in the long run, would it?

4. What we do with the teeth is a trade secret and I'm not allowed to tell you – sorry.

5. We don't do any other paid work except collecting teeth, but we do some voluntary work. My voluntary work is for the Lost Toothbrush

Programme. Tooth fairies check that you have a suitable toothbrush and that it's in good condition (for obvious reasons – we don't want dirty teeth!). If we find a toothbrush that needs replacing, we 'lose' it for you so your mum buys another. But don't tell anyone about that.

I have learnt to read and write English but it is not my first language – we tooth fairies have our own language. But, yes, tooth fairies can work anywhere and don't need a permit. There is a worldwide network of tooth fairies and how they work depends on the child they are working with, not the country. That's why you get the same money if your tooth falls out when you're on holiday! If you go to an area where teeth are cheaper, you will still get your usual rate. (But if you go somewhere teeth are more expensive, you might get more – that's up to the local fairy.) I hope this information is useful.

Yours magically
TF

IT'S A FACT
In the Middle Ages, children had to throw their shed teeth into the fire or bury them in the ground to prevent witches stealing them and having power over them (over the children, not the teeth). Getting money for shed teeth goes back to at least early Viking times!

Dear tooth fairy
How much does a child get in total, and what happens
if a tooth goes missing – do I still get the money? And
can you use a computer? I'd like to email you my stuff.
Love
Max

Dear Max

You can email me at molly@toothfairy.co.uk. This is fine
for messages, but please don't send big attachments as our
connection is slow. If you like, you can leave your computer turned
on and I can drop by and look at your stuff in the night when you're
asleep. You can work out how much a child gets in total, as you
know the rates for different teeth. A child who hasn't asked for more
gets 1 euro per tooth. If a tooth goes missing you should still get the
money – we can usually find them. If you swallow it – this is yukky
– we recover it from the sewage system. We have a tooth trap
in place (but the sewage people don't know about it!).
All good wishes
TF

From: max@velcroslug.com
To: molly@toothfairy.co.uk
Subject: Numbers for project

Hi TF, I've made a spreadsheet to work out the total you give for one child. Would you check it please? I used an average of 2.75 euros for the back teeth. In the bottom row, I used a formula to multiply the number of teeth by the price, then added them all up at the end of the row. Is this right? Do you keep track of each child's remaining teeth? M :-)

> **IT'S A FACT**
> If you need the same formula in several cells, you can copy it. The computer will alter the formula as it needs to — so if you copy the formula in B4 (=B2*B3) into C4, the computer will alter it to =C2*C3.

	A	B	C	D	E
1		Incisors	Canines	Molars	
2	No of teeth	8	4	4	
3	Price each	1	2	2.75	
4	Total (euros)	8	8	22	38

From: molly@toothfairy.co.uk
To: max@velcroslug.com
Subject: Re: Numbers for project

Yes, this is right — well done! We have a database that tracks how many teeth each child has left. We can use this to find out who's only got molars left, when we're likely to get more canines, and all sorts of useful stuff. Attached is a copy of your record! TF x

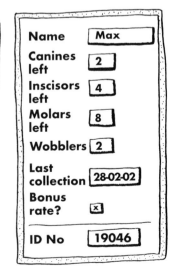

Name   Max
Canines left   2
Inscisors left   4
Molars left   8
Wobblers   2
Last collection   28-02-02
Bonus rate?   ☒
ID No   19046

From: max@velcroslug.com
To: molly@toothfairy.co.uk
Subject: Draft project

Hello tooth fairy :-)

Do you have a mobile phone? I've got to go to granny's at the weekend and she doesn't have a computer, but I'm taking my phone. I've done my project. Wow, tooth fairy, if we went to the bank with a business plan for your business we'd no way get any money! You could do better, you know.

Could you have a look at what I've done, please?

I've left it on my desk. Thanks :-)

Love – Max

From: molly@toothfairy.co.uk
To: max@velcroslug.com
Subject: Re: Draft project

Get real, Max! Tooth fairies don't have mobile phones! Have you ever seen one small enough for us? And would we want kids phoning up all the time saying 'My tooth's come out, where's my money? No way.

As for your project, this is a good start. You've got the facts right, but you could make it look a lot more exciting. Why not put some pictures in it and divide it up into sections? How about moving the stuff about what we do to the start? It would make a good introduction.

Do you have to give it in on paper? Could you maybe do a website or some multimedia? Just an idea.

TF x

PS Tooth fairies don't usually do consultancy on homework – don't get any ideas here! And thanks for pointing out our lack of profit. It's true we don't make much money – we do it for the love of it, you know!

From: max@velcroslug.com
To: molly@toothfairy.co.uk
Subject: Project again

Hello tooth fairy. Sorry about the mobile phone question. I'm off to granny's now, but I thought I'd just tell you I'm doing my project as a PowerPoint presentation instead – good idea, thanks! Do you know where I can get some good tooth fairy clip art? M :-

Yr project is Xcellent.
I've left a note on yr
desk 2 tell U where to
find 2th fairy clipart. U'll
C it when U get home :-)

From: max@velcroslug.com
To: molly@toothfairy.co.uk
Subject: Final project

Hello tooth fairy. I moved the text around like you suggested and I put the spreadsheet I made onto one of the slides, plus the picture you gave me of your database – thanks. I've put in some clip art, too, and a link to the tooth fairy home page and even a sound file that plays at the start (I recorded one of my sister's teeth shaking about in a box – hope you don't mind).
I've left it on screen on my desk. Please have a quick look through and see what you think.
Max :-)
PS My tooth fell out! :-D Please don't forget my 2 euros!!!!

BUSINESS MODEL PROJECT

for more info visit the Tooth Fairy website

The Business

Tooth fairies collect shed teeth and leave money in exchange.

Raw Material

Each child has 20 milk teeth. These are shed between the ages of 5 and 15.

Cost of teeth

Most children receive 1 euro per tooth. They can ask for a bonus.

Problems

Schedules can't be fixed because fairies don't know when teeth will fall out.

Advantages

There is guaranteed supply – all childrens' milk teeth fall out.

TF Database

A typical record:

Improvement

Add to the database:
• which teeth have been shed and when.
• a wobble rating for loose teeth.

To:	molly@toothfairy.co.uk
Cc:	
Subject:	Final project

Thanks a million, tooth fairy! I got a special award for my presentation – and I couldn't have done it without your help. You're a star :-)
Hope to see you soon!
Max xx

QUIZ TIME

N ow, to make sure you've been paying attention, here's a quiz to test your media mind!

1 Why check your work if you've got a spell checker? Well... which of these mistakes would it pick up?
a) Gorillas have hare all over they're bodies.
b) A poodle is a type of god.
c) My bycicle is rusty.
d) I eat baked beans out of the cane.

2 Where might you find a number in a field?
a) on a poster
b) in a spreadsheet
c) on a number farm
d) in a database

3 Which program would you use to create a slide show?
a) Excel
b) Outlook
c) PowerPoint
d) Word

4 You record the percentage of the population killed by sharks, snakes and mosquitoes each year. What is the best way to present the information?
a) as a list
b) as a line graph
c) as a pictogram
d) as a pie chart

5 Which of these can't you include on a web page?
a) a table with pictures in it
b) a link to a piece of music
c) a moving picture
d) a button to record what someone says

6 What's a brainstorm?
a) a bad headache
b) a thinking session where you write down all your ideas
c) a grown-up tantrum
d) a way of planning a website

7 Someone used Find and Replace on this bit of writing and they weren't careful enough about what they asked it to replace. Can you work out what has been found and what it's been replaced with?

Eggggs aregg an eggxcegglleggnt sourcegg of proteggin, eggspeggcially useggful if you aregg a vegggeggtarian.

ANSWERS

MEDIA ACTION

Practise your media skills and check what you've learnt by having a go at these fun projects!

LIFE SWAP!

Some people swap their homes to get a free holiday somewhere new. But wouldn't it be cool if you could swap your life with someone else's, just for a day or a week? Problem is, to get them to want to swap, you've got to make your life sound really exciting. (OK, if it was that exciting you wouldn't want to swap it – but just imagine...) Could you sell your life? Think about it!

Make a web page – or just design one using your word processor if you haven't got any web designing software – advertising your life for a swap. Don't forget to put in pictures of yourself, your house, your pets – anything that will make people really want to try your life!

CHANGE YOUR LIFE!
(For one week only)

Search for a life: [   ] Search

Back to home page

Option 276: Luki, Greenland

Hi, I'm Luki and I live in Greenland on a polar bear reserve. It's great fun, and not many people are eaten by the polar bears!

Come and feed my pet seal, Angeline, with fish – she likes a lot!

I'd like to go somewhere hot for a change!

Swap your life for Luki's:

Enter your email address here: [   ]

Magazine Mogul

If you want to be a great writer, you'd better start practising early. Why not create a magazine with your mates? You can prepare all your articles and stories on the computer using a word processor, get some pictures (find them on the web, do them on the computer or scan them in) and design your pages.

You can do the whole thing on the computer if you've got a desktop publishing program, or a word processor that lets you put your words and pictures where you like on the page. Alternatively, you could print them out, then cut them up and stick them onto paper in the right places. If you're going to do this, find out how to do your stories in narrow text columns so that you can stick more than one column of text on the page, just like a real newspaper or magazine. Don't forget to print big, eye-catching headlines.

You could do a magazine every month, or every term, to keep everyone up to date with what you're doing, what's cool and what's happening.

MANAGE YOUR MESS

Have you got a collection that's getting out of hand? It could be anything – CDs, trading cards, sugar packets, Gameboy games... Make a database to keep track of them and have all that vital info at your fingertips. Don't forget you need to keep adding new records each time you add to your collection – and make changes to the old records if anything changes. (OK, your CDs aren't suddenly going to get new tracks – but you might make progress on your Gameboy game or swap some of your cards.)

CHRISTMAS CRACKER

Next Christmas, impress Santa with a presentation for a Christmas list! You can find pictures of the things you want, and even put in links to websites where they can be ordered. You can get lots of Christmas clip art to make it look really festive – do a search for "clip art" +Christmas +kids.

GRAPHS 'N' CHARTS

A boy watched birds in his garden for a day and saw:
4 blackbirds, 2 robins, 3 blue tits, 1 magpie, 6 starlings.
Draw two different graphs to show what he saw. Make them look as interesting as possible, and as easy to understand as you can.

Spot the Mistakes

If you don't check your work properly, you could end up with some pretty weird results – like these! See if you can spot what's gone wrong.

1 Can you find nine mistakes that the spell check has missed?

> At the weekend I went to the zoo with me dad. We went by train but my little sister was worried the rain would crash. I said their were hardly ever cashes but she still cried. At the zoo, an elephant sprayed water at my dad and he got all went. It was very funny. We had an ice cream in the after noon but my sister drop hers and cried again. Its so annoying – she always crying.

2 Some spell checkers will suggest correct spellings for you – but make sure they're offering you the right word first. See if you can work out what this document should say. The first version shows what was typed in. The second version shows you how it looked after the spell checker had tried to fix it.

> My bet fiend has a lot of badgrs in his acket. He gpt theme from all over the wrd, on his holdays. Hs vest ome is form the Grand Canon.
> It jus shos a big whole in the groundh.

> My bet fiend has a lot of badgers in his packet. He gut theme from all over the word, on his holidays. His vest omen is form the Grand Canon. It jut shops a big whole in the groundhog.

ANSWERS

1 It should say:

> At the weekend I went to the zoo with **my** dad. We went by train but my little sister was worried the **train** would crash. I said **there** were hardly ever **crashes** but she still cried. At the zoo, an elephant sprayed water at my dad and he got all **wet**. It was very funny. We had an ice cream in the **afternoon** but my sister **dropped** hers and cried again. **It's** so annoying – **she's** always crying.

The spell checker can't tell if you've used the wrong word for what you're trying to say. (But if your word processor has a grammar checker as well, this might spot some of the mistakes.)

2 It should say:

> My best friend has a lot of badges on his jacket. He got them from all over the world, on his holidays. His best one is from the Grand Canyon. It just shows a big hole in the ground.

The spell checker replaces a word that is spelt wrongly with one that it thinks is the closest match – its solution is not always the word you had in mind!

JAZZY BITS

Why not spice up your work by downloading some of these fab bits and pieces from the Internet?

CLIP ART AND MOVING PICTURES

★ www.kidsdomain.com/clip
★ www.thekidzpage.com/freeclipart.htm
★ www.webplaces.com/html/clipart.htm
★ www.awesomeclipartforkids.com
★ www.animfactory.com
★ www.snowcrest.net/kitty/hpages

or search for "clip art" +kids

BACKGROUND PATTERNS, BORDERS AND BUTTONS

http://theboutique.org
★ www.backgroundcity.com
★ www.coolarchive.com/backgrounds.cfm
★ www.grsites.com/textures
★ www.coolarchive.com/buttons.cfm – make your own buttons online.

FONTS

★ http://fonts.tom7.com
★ www.chank.com/freefonts.php
★ www.speakeasy.org/~ecf/freeware.html

MEDIA MADNESS

★ EARLY NEWS

The oldest newspaper is said to be the Korean *Cho-bo* which was first printed in the 15th century. It had political news and information about the weather and was printed every day. It didn't have any TV listings though!

★ SCREEN SURPISES

Bored programmers writing software often hide something sneaky in the finished program. They're called 'easter eggs' and you sometimes come across them if you press random combinations of keys or click on odd areas of the screen. (But beware – save your work first, as sometimes this might crash your machine. Doh!)

★ CODE CRACKING

The earliest word processors didn't show you on screen what you would get on the printed page. Instead, you saw a whole lot of codes and funny character sequences that told you what was going on. So this is bold would tell you a bit of text was in bold. Complicated!

★ STICKY SITUATION

Before the 1980s, the only way to get text and pictures on the same page in your document was to print out both, cut them up with scissors and glue them onto a new page. This is where the cut and paste icons and the term 'clipboard' (to hold the cut out bits) come from.

It'll just have to do!

★ A WRITE HASSLE

Life's much easier with a word processor. Until the late 20th century, a writer who wanted to make changes to his or her book had to type it again. And before the end of the 19th century, they had to write it out by hand again. Bet that stopped them moving bits around!

★ ANCIENT LETTERS

Printing was first done with pieces of metal, one for each letter, which were combined to make up words and lines of text. This started around 1455 when the letters looked rather like the handwriting of the time. But different fonts were being developed by the end of the 15th century that started to look like our fonts. Some of the fonts you can use on your computer today are hundreds of years old!

GLOSSARY

CELL A space on a spreadsheet to hold a number, label or formula.

DATABASE A collection of records holding information about things or people.

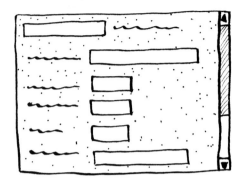

DESKTOP PUBLISHING A computer program for arranging words and pictures on pages.

DOWNLOAD To copy something from the Internet onto your own computer.

EDIT To make changes to a document.

FIELD A space for information on a database record.

FONT A style of lettering.

IMPORT To copy a picture or other file into a document, web page or presentation.

INTERNET A worldwide network connecting millions of computers.

MULTIMEDIA A document or file that combines different types of information, such as pictures, words, sounds, and video.

Wow!

PRESENTATION (in PowerPoint, for example) A set of slides to look at on the computer or show using an overhead projector.

QUERY A question you ask a database about the info you've put in.

RECORD A set of information in a database.

REPORT A display or printout of info. In a database it is often the answer to a query.

SLIDE SHOW A set of slides made into a presentation you can run on your computer.

SORT To put information into order in a list, spreadsheet or database.

SPREADSHEET A computer program for working with numbers eg doing calculations and trying out different numbers in these calculations.

	A	B	C
1			
2			
3			
4			
5			

TABLE A set of information arranged in rows and columns, or a whole set of records in a database.

If you find any more words you don't know, look them up at www.webopedia.com – an online dictionary of computer and Internet terms.

INDEX